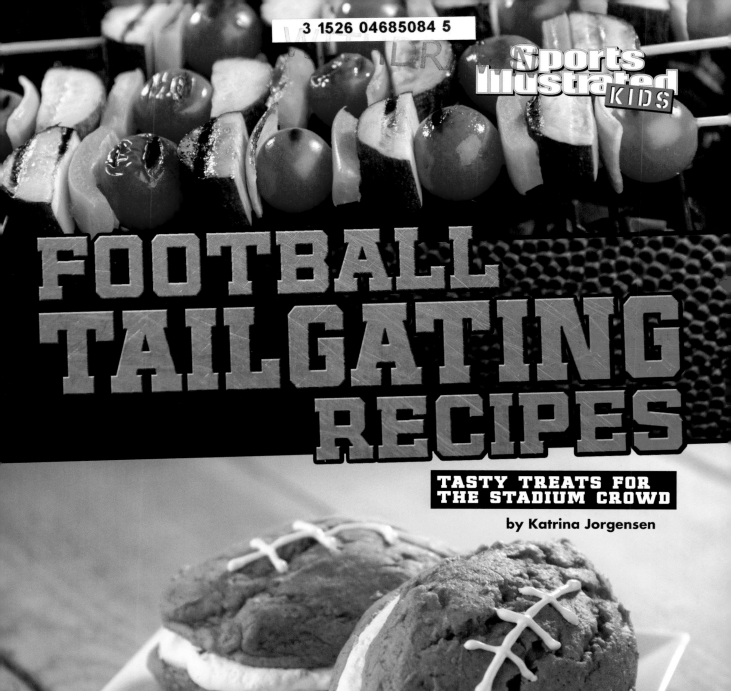

Sports Illustrated KIDS

FOOTBALL TAILGATING RECIPES

TASTY TREATS FOR THE STADIUM CROWD

by Katrina Jorgensen

CAPSTONE PRESS
a capstone imprint

Sports Illustrated Kids Football Cookbooks are published by Capstone Press,
1710 Roe Crest Drive, North Mankato, Minnesota 56003.
www.capstonepub.com

Library of Congress Cataloging-in-Publication Data
Jorgensen, Katrina, author.
  Football tailgating recipes : tasty treats for the stadium crowd / by
Katrina Jorgensen.
      pages cm.—(Sports illustrated kids. Football cookbooks)
  Summary: "A fun football cookbook with recipes for food to make on the
go for the tailgating crowd."—Provided by publisher.
  Audience: Ages 9-15.
  Audience: Grades 4 to 6.
  Includes bibliographical references.
  ISBN 978-1-4914-2137-6 (library binding)
1. Outdoor cooking—Juvenile literature. 2. Tailgate parties—Juvenile literature.
I. Title.
  TX823.J67 2015
  641.5'78—dc23   2014034069

Editorial Credits
Anthony Wacholtz, editor; Kyle Grenz, designer; Eric Gohl, media researcher;
Laura Manthe, production specialist; Marcy Morin, scheduler; Sarah Schuette,
food stylist

Photo Credits
All images by Capstone Studio: Karon Dubke. Author photo by
STILLCODA Photography.

The author dedicates this book to her parents, Knud and Brigitte,
for their support in everything she does.

Printed in Canada.
092014   008478FRS15

TABLE OF CONTENTS

Score a Touchdown With Your Tailgating Party!

Set up your chairs and lower the tailgate! It's time to party with the ultimate collection of tailgating grub and goodies. Draft your top picks to form the perfect team of snacks, main courses, treats, and beverages. Get started by gathering the supplies and ingredients. See each recipe for the full list of what you'll need to kick off your cooking.

COOKING 101

PREP TIME	the amount of time it takes to prepare ingredients before cooking
INACTIVE PREP TIME	the amount of time it takes to indirectly prepare ingredients before cooking, such as allowing dough to rise
COOK TIME	the amount of time it takes to cook a recipe after preparing the ingredients

Conversions

Using metric tools? No problem!
Here are measurement conversions to make your recipe measure up.

Temperature

Fahrenheit	Celsius
325°	160°
350°	180°
375°	190°
400°	200°
425°	220°
450°	230°

Measurements

1/4 teaspoon	1.25 grams or milliliters
1/2 teaspoon	2.5 g or mL
1 teaspoon	5 g or mL
1 tablespoon	15 g or mL
1/4 cup	57 g (dry) or 60 mL (liquid)
1/3 cup	75 g (dry) or 80 mL (liquid)
1/2 cup	114 g (dry) or 125 mL (liquid)
2/3 cup	150 g (dry) or 160 mL (liquid)
3/4 cup	170 g (dry) or 175 mL (liquid)
1 cup	227 g (dry) or 240 mL (liquid)
1 quart	950 mL

blend—to mix together, sometimes using a blender

boil—to heat until large bubbles form on top of a liquid; the boiling point for water is 212°F (100°C)

chop—to cut into small pieces with a knife

dissolve—to incorporate a solid food into a liquid by melting or stirring

grate—to cut into small strips using a grater

knead—to mix dough by flattening it with the heel of your hand, folding it in half, pressing down again, and repeating several times; use flour on your work surface to prevent the dough from sticking

mash—to smash a soft food into a lumpy mixture

preheat—to turn the oven on ahead of time so it reaches the correct temperature before you are ready to bake

simmer—to cook foods in hot liquids kept just below the boiling point of water

slice—to cut into thin pieces with a knife

spread—to put a thin layer of a soft food onto another food

thaw—to bring frozen food to room temperature

Keep your eyes open for helpful and creative sidebars throughout the book. Switch up your recipes with Call an Audible ideas, and get insight from the expert with Coach's Tips!

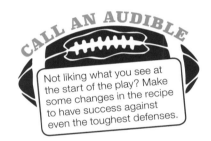

CALL AN AUDIBLE

Not liking what you see at the start of the play? Make some changes in the recipe to have success against even the toughest defenses.

COACH'S TIP

Gain the edge in the kitchen with these cool tips, tricks, and techniques.

Tailgating Tips

All of the recipes in this book can either be made at home or finished off at the game. Steps numbered in orange highlight what you need to do to finish the big play at the stadium.

Safety in the Kitchen

You can have fun in the kitchen and be safe too. Always start your recipes with clean hands, tools, and surfaces. Make sure you wash your hands and keep your tools and surfaces clean after handling raw meat. Use your knife carefully. Ask an adult for help when cutting food or handling hot dishes.

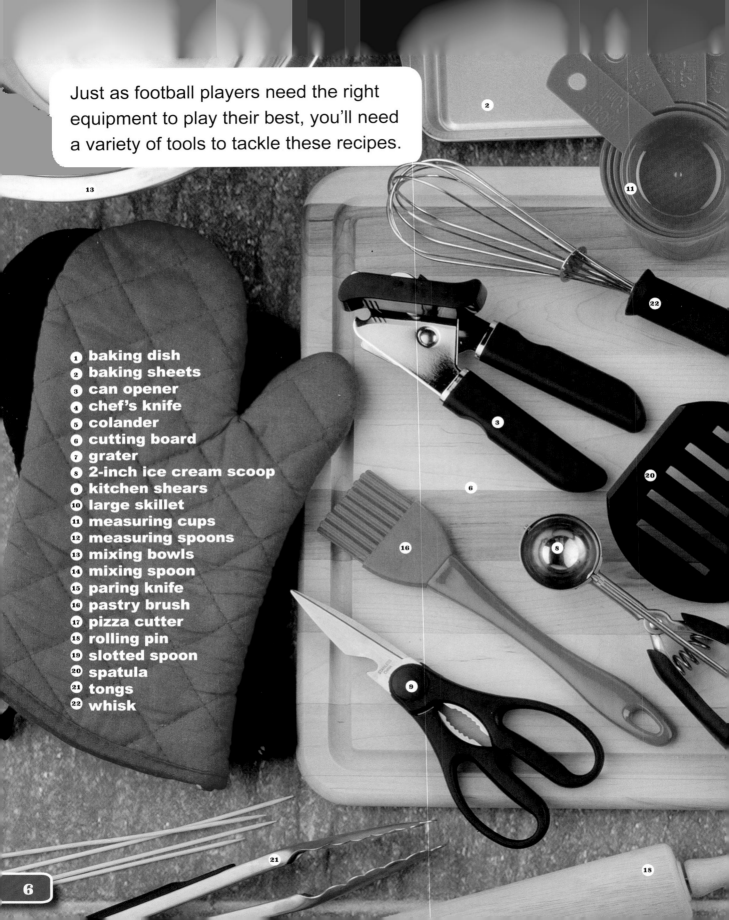

Just as football players need the right equipment to play their best, you'll need a variety of tools to tackle these recipes.

1. baking dish
2. baking sheets
3. can opener
4. chef's knife
5. colander
6. cutting board
7. grater
8. 2-inch ice cream scoop
9. kitchen shears
10. large skillet
11. measuring cups
12. measuring spoons
13. mixing bowls
14. mixing spoon
15. paring knife
16. pastry brush
17. pizza cutter
18. rolling pin
19. slotted spoon
20. spatula
21. tongs
22. whisk

SWEET POTATO CHIPS

Instead of cracking open a bag of chips, bring some delicious homemade potato chips to the stadium!

PREP TIME	10 MINUTES
COOK TIME	30 MINUTES
SERVES	4 TO 6 PEOPLE

Tools

- baking sheet
- parchment paper
- chef's knife
- cutting board
- 2 mixing bowls
- spatula
- bowl scraper

Ingredients

For the chips:

- 2 medium sweet potatoes
- 1 teaspoon salt
- ½ teaspoon pepper
- 1 teaspoon brown sugar
- ¼ teaspoon cinnamon
- 3 tablespoons olive oil

For the dip:

- 1 chipotle pepper in adobo sauce
- 1 lime
- 1 cup sour cream

1 Preheat the oven to 450ºF. Line a baking sheet with parchment paper and set aside.

2 Scrub the sweet potatoes clean and pat dry.

3 Carefully slice sweet potatoes into ¼-inch rounds. Place the rounds in a large mixing bowl.

4 Add remaining ingredients for the chips to the bowl. Toss the ingredients to coat the potatoes with oil and spices.

COACH'S TIP

Find chipotle peppers in adobo sauce in the Mexican food aisle at your local grocery store. They are usually canned or jarred. Save the leftovers in a container in your refrigerator for up to two weeks. Use them in chili, salsa, or any Mexican dish you like!

5 Pour the contents of the bowl on the baking sheet and spread it out. Make sure the potatoes are flat and not stacked on top of each other.

6 Bake for about 15 minutes. Remove the baking sheet from the oven and flip the potatoes over using a spatula.

7 Bake another 15 minutes or until the potatoes are crisp. Remove from the oven and let cool before placing in a bowl for serving.

For the dip:

1 On a clean cutting board, chop the chipotle pepper into very small pieces.

2 Slice the lime in half and squeeze the juice into a small mixing bowl, making sure no seeds fall in.

3 Add the chopped pepper and sour cream.

4 Stir well and place in a small serving bowl alongside the sweet potato chips for dipping.

CHEESY JALAPEÑO CORNBREAD MUFFINS

For an appetizer with a kick, cheesy jalapeño cornbread muffins are a sure crowd-pleaser!

PREP TIME	**15** MINUTES
COOK TIME	**20 TO 22** MINUTES
MAKES	**12** MUFFINS

Tools
- cutting board
- chef's knife
- grater
- 2 mixing bowls
- measuring cups/ spoons
- small saucepan
- spoon
- whisk
- 12 muffin liners
- muffin pan
- toothpick

Ingredients
- 3 tablespoons pickled jalapeños
- 1 cup sharp cheddar cheese
- 1¼ cup finely ground cornmeal
- 1 cup all-purpose flour
- 2½ teaspoons baking powder
- ½ teaspoon salt
- ¼ cup butter
- ⅓ cup honey
- 1 cup buttermilk
- 2 large eggs
- 8 ounces frozen corn

1 Preheat oven to 375ºF.

2 Chop the jalapeños very finely and set aside.

3 Grate the cheddar cheese and set aside.

4 Combine the cornmeal, flour, baking powder, and salt in a mixing bowl.

5 Melt the butter over low heat in the saucepan and set aside.

6 In a second mixing bowl, whisk together the honey, buttermilk, eggs, and melted butter.

7 Pour the liquid ingredients into the dry ingredients and stir until just combined.

8 Stir in the cheese, corn, and jalapeños.

9 Place muffin liners into the muffin pan and scoop batter into the liners. Fill two-thirds full.

10 Bake for 20 to 22 minutes or until a toothpick inserted into a muffin comes out clean.

11 Serve warm or at room temperature.

COACH'S TIP

Make them bite-sized by using a mini-muffin pan! Spray the cups of a mini-muffin pan with cooking spray and fill each three-fourths full. Bake for about 15 minutes or until a toothpick inserted comes out clean.

GRILLED POTATO WEDGES

Ready for a two-minute drill? That's how long it will take for you and your friends to devour these wedges!

PREP TIME	**10** MINUTES
COOK TIME	**20** MINUTES
SERVES	**4 TO 6 PEOPLE**

Tools
- 2 mixing bowls
- measuring cups/spoons
- spoon
- cutting board
- chef's knife
- 2 trays or baking sheets
- tongs
- grill

Ingredients
- 3 large baking potatoes
- 1 teaspoon paprika
- 1 teaspoon dried oregano
- 1 teaspoon garlic salt
- ½ teaspoon pepper
- ½ cup olive oil, divided

1 Scrub the potatoes clean and pat dry.

2 Combine the paprika, oregano, garlic salt, and pepper in a small mixing bowl and set aside.

3 Cut each potato into eight pieces by cutting it in half lengthwise. Then cut each half lengthwise again into four wedges.

4 Place potato wedges in a second mixing bowl with half the oil. Toss to coat the potatoes with oil. Place potatoes on a tray or baking sheet and set aside.

5 Heat the grill to 375°F on one side. If you're using a charcoal grill, move the hot charcoal to one side of the grill. Carefully oil the grill grates with the remaining oil.

CALL AN AUDIBLE

Sub in any firm vegetable for the potatoes, such as sweet potato or zucchini.

6 Place the wedges on the grill directly over the heat. Cook until browned on all sides for about 2 to 3 minutes per side, using tongs to turn.

7 Once the wedges are browned on all sides, move them to the side without heat. Close the grill for about 10 to 15 minutes or until the wedges are tender.

8 Use tongs to remove the potatoes from the grill. Place on a clean tray or baking sheet and sprinkle on the seasonings. Serve hot.

GRILLED CORN

Listen up! Your friends won't want to pass on these ears. Try out these grilled cobs for the perfect side for your tailgating party.

PREP TIME | 45 MINUTES (30 MINUTES INACTIVE)

COOK TIME | 20 MINUTES

SERVES | 6 PEOPLE

Tools
- large mixing bowl
- saucepan
- cutting board
- chef's knife
- grill
- small mixing bowl
- tongs
- pastry brush

Ingredients
- 6 ears of sweet corn
- water for soaking the corn
- 2 cloves garlic
- ½ stick butter

1. Peel back the husks from the corn but don't remove them. Remove the silk (the stringy stuff inside).

2. Fold the husks back and place the ears in a large mixing bowl with enough water to cover. Let them soak for 30 minutes.

3. Meanwhile, make the garlic butter: Chop the garlic finely and melt the butter in a saucepan over medium heat. Add garlic and let it sizzle until fragrant. Remove from heat right away to avoid burning.

4. Heat grill to 375ºF. Put the corn on the grill and cook for about 15 minutes, turning the ears three or four times using tongs.

COACH'S TIP
Avoid burns when removing the husks from the hot corn. Use an old kitchen towel to get a comfortable hold on each ear as you remove the husks after grilling.

5 Use tongs to remove the corn from the grill, but leave the heat on. Remove the husks from the ears of corn. Use a pastry brush to cover the corn with garlic butter.

6 Put the corn back on the grill using tongs. Grill an additional 1 to 2 minutes per side or until some of the kernels are browned. Serve warm immediately.

BAKED BEANS

Shake off the shivers during a chilly fall football game with a piping hot bowl of baked beans.

PREP TIME | **10 MINUTES**

COOK TIME | **1 HOUR**

SERVES | **8 PEOPLE**

Tools

- cutting board
- chef's knife
- sauté pan
- spoon
- 9 x 13-inch baking dish

Ingredients

- 1 small onion
- 3 slices thick-cut bacon
- 1 tablespoon butter
- ¼ cup barbecue sauce
- 2 tablespoons brown sugar
- 1 teaspoon dry mustard
- 2 16-ounce cans pork and beans

1 Preheat oven to 350ºF.

2 Chop the onion finely and set aside.

3 Cube the bacon into ½-inch pieces and set aside.

4 In a large sauté pan, heat the butter over medium heat.

5 Add the bacon and onion to the sauté pan. Sauté for about 5 minutes or until the onions have softened slightly. Stir in the remaining ingredients.

6 Pour the contents of the sauté pan into the baking dish.

7 Bake in the oven for about one hour and serve warm.

CALL AN AUDIBLE

Vegetarians can skip the bacon! Instead add 1 tablespoon soy sauce for extra flavor.

PRIMAVERA PASTA SALAD

A variety of flavorful ingredients come together in this Pro Bowl salad.

PREP TIME | **30 MINUTES**

COOK TIME | **2 HOURS** (1 HOUR 30 MINUTES INACTIVE)

SERVES | **8 PEOPLE**

Tools

- large stockpot
- measuring cups/ spoons
- chef's knife
- cutting board
- colander
- 2 mixing bowls
- whisk
- scraper
- serving bowl

Ingredients

- 2 tablespoons salt
- 1 pound penne pasta
- 6 spears asparagus
- ½ cup frozen peas
- 3 tablespoons olive oil
- ½ cup cherry tomatoes
- ½ cup grated carrots
- 1 heart of romaine lettuce
- ½ cup olives (optional)

For the sauce:

- ¾ cup plain Greek yogurt
- 3 tablespoons olive oil
- 1 teaspoon lemon juice
- 2 teaspoons garlic, minced
- 2 teaspoons Worcestershire sauce
- ⅓ cup grated Parmesan cheese

1 Fill a large stockpot three-fourths full with water and add salt. Once the water is boiling, add the pasta. Reduce the heat slightly to avoid boiling over. Boil for about 10 minutes or until the pasta is tender but still firm to bite.

2 While the pasta is cooking, chop the asparagus into 1-inch pieces. When the pasta has about 5 minutes left to boil, add the asparagus to the pot. After 3 more minutes, add the frozen peas.

3 Drain the pasta, asparagus, and peas into the colander and run cold water over it to stop the cooking process.

4 Empty the colander into a mixing bowl and drizzle olive oil over the pasta and vegetables. Toss the mixture to coat with oil. Place in the refrigerator to cool while you prepare the other ingredients.

5 Cut the tomatoes in half. Chop the lettuce into bite-sized pieces. Set aside.

6 For the dressing: In a small mixing bowl, combine the yogurt, olive oil, lemon juice, garlic, Worcestershire sauce, and Parmesan cheese.

7 When the pasta and vegetables have cooled, add the tomatoes, lettuce, carrots, olives, and dressing to the mixing bowl. With a scraper, stir to combine the ingredients.

COACH'S TIP

Just like a coach who knows when to sub in the right players, a good chef knows the right balance of ingredients. But sometimes it takes a little experimentation to get it just right. When making the dressing, use more water to thin the dressing if it's too thick. If the dressing is too thin, add yogurt.

8 Pour into a serving bowl, cover, and refrigerate for at least 1½ hours before serving.

HONEY-LIME COLESLAW

Don't leave this tasty coleslaw on the bench! You can put the creamy mixture on burgers, tacos, and sandwiches too.

PREP TIME | **45 MINUTES**

COOK TIME | **1 HOUR** (1 HOUR INACTIVE)

SERVES | **6 PEOPLE**

Tools

- cutting board
- chef's knife
- mixing bowl
- measuring cup/spoon
- whisk

Ingredients

- ½ cup olive oil
- 3 tablespoons honey
- 2 limes, sliced in half
- 1 teaspoon salt
- 1 teaspoon pepper
- 2 teaspoons ground cumin
- ½ small red onion
- 1-pound package coleslaw mix (shredded cabbage and carrots)

1 Make the dressing: Whisk together the olive oil, honey, juice of the limes, salt, pepper, and cumin in a large mixing bowl.

2 Thinly slice the red onion. Add to the mixing bowl.

3 Add coleslaw mix and toss gently to coat.

4 Cover and store in refrigerator for 1 hour before serving.

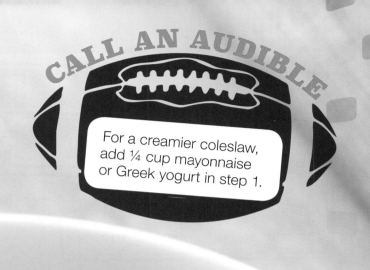

CALL AN AUDIBLE

For a creamier coleslaw, add ¼ cup mayonnaise or Greek yogurt in step 1.

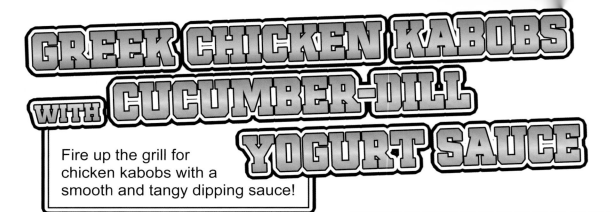

GREEK CHICKEN KABOBS WITH CUCUMBER-DILL YOGURT SAUCE

Fire up the grill for chicken kabobs with a smooth and tangy dipping sauce!

PREP TIME	**1 HOUR 30 MINUTES** (1 HOUR INACTIVE)
COOK TIME	**15 MINUTES**
SERVES	**4 TO 6 PEOPLE**

Tools

- 8 10-inch wooden skewers
- 2 shallow rectangular baking dishes
- 2 mixing bowls
- whisk
- cutting board
- knife
- gallon-sized ziptop bag
- grill
- tongs
- grater

Ingredients

- 1 pound boneless, skinless chicken breasts

For the marinade:

- ½ cup olive oil
- ¼ cup lemon juice
- 1 teaspoon dried oregano
- 1 teaspoon dried rosemary
- 1 teaspoon dried thyme
- 1 teaspoon salt
- ½ teaspoon pepper

For the cucumber-dill yogurt sauce:

- 1 cup plain low-fat or Greek yogurt
- 1 teaspoon dried dill
- 1 tablespoon lemon juice
- ½ English cucumber
- salt and pepper

1 Place the skewers in a shallow baking dish with enough water to cover. Soak for 20 minutes while you prepare the meat and marinade.

2 Place the marinade ingredients in a mixing bowl and whisk to combine. Place the ingredients in the ziptop bag, seal, and set aside.

3 Cut chicken breasts into 1-inch chunks.

4 Place the chicken in the bag and seal. Squish the chicken around in the liquid to cover.

5 Put the bag in a shallow baking dish in the refrigerator. Allow to marinate for at least 1 hour. Marinate for up to 8 hours if preparing ahead of time.

6 After the chicken is done marinating, thread the chicken on the skewers and place in the clean baking dish.

7 Heat the grill to 400°F. Place skewers carefully on grill for about 5 minutes on each side, or until cooked.

8 Serve with cucumber-dill yogurt sauce.

For the cucumber-dill yogurt sauce:

1 Place the yogurt, dill, and lemon juice in a bowl.

2 Grate the cucumber.

3 Add the cucumber to the bowl and stir well.

4 Add salt and pepper a pinch at a time until it tastes just right.

VEGETABLE KABOBS WITH HERB RANCH SAUCE

You don't need meat to make a mean kabob! Stack up the veggies and start up the grill for this tailgating treat.

PREP TIME	**1 HOUR 30 MINUTES** (1 HOUR INACTIVE)
COOK TIME	**10 MINUTES**
SERVES	**6 TO 8 PEOPLE**

Tools

- 8 10-inch wooden skewers
- shallow rectangular baking dish
- cutting board
- chef's knife
- tray or baking sheet
- pastry brush
- measuring cups/spoons
- mixing bowl
- scraper

Ingredients

- 1 zucchini
- 2 bell peppers
- 1 small red onion
- 1 pound cherry tomatoes
- ¼ cup olive oil
- 1 teaspoon salt
- ½ teaspoon pepper

For the herb ranch sauce:

- ½ cup plain low-fat or Greek yogurt
- ⅓ cup buttermilk
- ¼ teaspoon garlic powder
- ¼ teaspoon onion powder
- ¼ teaspoon dried thyme
- ¼ teaspoon dried dill
- ½ teaspoon dried parsley
- salt and pepper

1 Place the skewers in the shallow baking dish with enough water to cover. Soak for 20 minutes while you prepare the vegetables.

2 Cut the zucchini in half lengthwise. Then cut into half-moons by cutting across in 1-inch pieces.

3 Cut the peppers in half. Then cut each half into four pieces.

4 Peel and cut the onion in half lengthwise, then widthwise. Peel several layers and set aside.

COACH'S TIP

Cutting peppers can be tricky, but follow these tips and you'll look like a pro. First cut the pepper on top to remove the stem. Then cut it in half lengthwise, from stem to bottom. Scoop out the seeds and pith (the white fibrous veins running up and down the pepper). Then you're set to cut it into the sizes you need!

5 Thread the skewers with zucchini, onions, bell peppers, and tomatoes until the skewers are full. Set the finished skewers on a tray or baking sheet.

6 Using a pastry brush, paint all sides of the vegetables with olive oil, then season with salt and pepper.

7 Heat grill to 400ºF. Carefully place skewers on the grill and cook 3 to 4 minutes per side.

8 Serve with herb ranch dipping sauce.

For the herb ranch sauce:

Combine all the sauce ingredients in a mixing bowl and stir well with a scraper. Allow to sit 10 minutes before serving.

BURGER SLIDER

Good (and delicious) things come in small packages!
Watch your friends send in a blitz for these miniature burgers.

PREP TIME	20 MINUTES
COOK TIME	15 MINUTES
MAKES	4 TO 6 PEOPLE

Tools

- cutting board
- chef's knife
- platter or large plate
- mixing bowl
- 2 trays or baking sheets
- grill
- spatula

Ingredients

- 2 pounds lean ground beef
- 1 tablespoon paprika
- 1½ teaspoons salt
- 1 teaspoon pepper
- 1 teaspoon onion flakes
- ¾ teaspoon garlic powder
- 8 slider buns
- your favorite burger toppings, such as cheese, lettuce, sliced tomatoes, onions, pickles, ketchup, or mustard

CALL AN AUDIBLE

Sliders come in many varieties! Sub in ground chicken or pork in place of ground beef. For a vegetarian option, sprinkle the seasonings on portabella mushrooms before grilling.

1 Prepare your toppings and arrange on a platter or large plate. Set aside.

2 Place the ground beef, paprika, salt, pepper, onion flakes, and garlic powder in a mixing bowl.

3 Using your hands, mix the meat well with the seasonings.

4 Separate the meat into 8 equal pieces.

5 Form round patties and place on a tray or baking sheet.

6 Heat the grill to 400°F.

7 Carefully place the patties on the grill and cook about 5 minutes per side or until fully cooked.

8 Transfer cooked burgers to a clean tray or baking sheet.

9 Place the burgers on slider buns, dress with fixings, and serve.

BARBECUED RIBS

Grab some napkins—it's going to get messy! Mouth-watering ribs paired with a savory BBQ sauce make a winning combination.

PREP TIME	**10** MINUTES
COOK TIME	**5 HOURS 20 MINUTES** (5 HOURS INACTIVE)
SERVES	**6** PEOPLE

Tools

- measuring cups/ spoons
- small mixing bowl
- cutting board
- heavy-duty aluminum foil
- baking sheet
- grill
- tongs
- pastry brush

Ingredients

- 2 racks baby back ribs, silver skin removed
- 1 cup barbecue sauce, plus more for serving

For the rib rub:

- $2/3$ cup brown sugar
- $1/4$ cup smoked paprika
- 2 tablespoons pepper
- 1 tablespoon kosher salt
- 1 tablespoon chili powder
- 1 tablespoon garlic powder
- 1 tablespoon onion powder
- 1 tablespoon dry mustard

COACH'S TIP

Know when your ribs are ready to make the transition from oven to grill. Carefully peel back a small part of the rib meat and stick a fork in. If you get no resistance, they're good to go. If it's a little hard to poke the fork in, give them some more time in the oven.

1 Preheat oven to 250°F.

2 Combine the rib rub ingredients in a small mixing bowl and stir to combine.

3 Place rib racks on the cutting board. Sprinkle the rib rub all over the racks, top and bottom.

4 Make foil packets by tearing two sheets of aluminum foil per rack that are slightly longer than the rib racks. Place the ribs on top of the first foil sheet. Then place the second foil sheet over the ribs and seal tightly. Repeat for the second rack of ribs.

5 Put the foil packets on a baking sheet and place in the oven. Bake for about 4 to 5 hours.

6 Heat grill to 450°F. Carefully remove the foil and use tongs to place the ribs on the grill.

7 Use a pastry brush to coat the ribs with barbecue sauce on all sides. Allow to cook for about 5 minutes on each side.

8 Remove the ribs from the grill. Serve immediately with additional sauce on the side.

HAWAIIAN BBQ CHICKEN BURGERS

Aloha! Bring a tropical twist to your tailgating party with these tasty chicken burgers.

PREP TIME	**20** MINUTES
COOK TIME	**15 TO 20** MINUTES
SERVES	**6** PEOPLE

Tools

- mixing bowl
- cutting board
- chef's knife
- measuring cups/spoons
- tray or baking sheet
- grill
- spatula

Ingredients

- 2 pounds ground chicken
- 1 teaspoon paprika
- 1 teaspoon cumin
- 1 teaspoon chili-garlic sauce
- 2 tablespoons soy sauce
- ½ teaspoon garlic powder
- ½ teaspoon salt
- 3 green onions
- oil for brushing on grill grates
- 6 pineapple rings
- 6 slices Monterey Jack cheese
- 6 hamburger buns
- barbecue sauce

1 Combine the ground chicken, paprika, cumin, chili-garlic sauce, soy sauce, garlic powder, and salt in a mixing bowl.

2 Finely chop enough green onions to make one-half cup. Add to the mixing bowl.

3 With your hands, mix the meat lightly with the seasonings and onions.

4 Evenly divide the meat mixture into six pieces. Form the meat into patties and place on a tray or baking sheet.

CALL AN AUDIBLE

Not everyone is a fan of spice! To tame the recipe down a bit, replace the paprika with 1 teaspoon onion powder and the chili-garlic sauce with 1 teaspoon barbecue sauce.

COACH'S TIP

Find chili-garlic sauce in the Asian aisle at the supermarket. It can be used in sauces, marinades, soups, or even as a topping on pizza. Be careful, though—a little goes a long way. It has a kick!

5 Heat the grill to 400°F. Lightly coat the grill grates with oil.

6 Place the patties on the grill and cook 7 to 8 minutes per side or until done.

7 While the patties are cooking, grill the pineapple for 1 to 2 minutes per side. Remove from the grill and set aside.

8 Put cheese slices on the chicken burgers when 1 minute of cooking time remains.

9 Using a spatula, carefully remove the chicken burgers from the grill and place on buns.

10 Place the pineapple on top of the burger and top with barbecue sauce.

11 Add the top bun and serve. Optional: Serve with grilled potato or zucchini wedges (see recipe on pages 12–13).

PULLED CHICKEN TACO BAR

Impress your friends and stifle their hunger by setting up a pulled chicken taco bar right at the stadium!

PREP TIME | **25 MINUTES**

COOK TIME | **4 HOURS** (4 HOURS INACTIVE)

SERVES | **6 PEOPLE**

Tools

- 3-quart slow cooker
- cutting board
- chef's knife
- aluminum foil
- small serving bowls and spoons

Ingredients

- 2 pounds boneless, skinless chicken thighs
- 1 15-ounce jar salsa
- 1 tablespoon chili powder
- 1 tablespoon ground cumin
- 1 tablespoon pepper
- 2 teaspoons salt
- 1½ cups cheese, grated
- 2 cups romaine or iceberg lettuce
- 2 tomatoes
- 1 small red onion
- 1 cup sour cream
- additional salsa for topping (optional)
- 12 flour or corn tortillas

1 Combine the chicken, salsa, chili powder, cumin, pepper, and salt in a slow cooker. Stir to combine and cook on low setting for 4 hours.

CALL AN AUDIBLE

If you don't want chicken on your roster, put pulled pork in the game. Use boneless pork shoulder and increase the cook time to 7 to 8 hours.

2 When the meat has 30 minutes left to cook, chop the lettuce and dice the tomatoes and onions. Place the cheese, lettuce, tomatoes, onions, sour cream, and extra salsa in small serving bowls with spoons.

3 When the chicken is done, place it on a cutting board and use two forks to shred the meat. Return to the slow cooker and turn the heat setting to warm.

4 Take slow cooker and toppings to the stadium. Place chicken on tortillas and add toppings.

COACH'S TIP

Taking all those serving bowls to the stadium might be tricky for your tailgating party. Instead, put your toppings in a muffin pan and cover it with foil. Simple to transport and easy to clean!

GRILLED FRUIT ICE CREAM SUNDAES

There's the whistle! It's time for dessert. With this unique sundae, you can combine ice cream and grilling!

PREP TIME | 15 MINUTES

COOK TIME | 15 MINUTES

SERVES | 4 PEOPLE

Ingredients

- various fruits, such as peaches, pineapple, apricots, watermelon, plums, or bananas
- ice cream

For the caramel sauce:

- 2 tablespoons unsalted butter
- ½ cup dark brown sugar
- ¼ cup half-and-half or heavy cream
- ½ teaspoon vanilla extract
- 1 pinch kosher salt

For the chocolate sauce:

- ½ cup semisweet chocolate chips
- ¼ cup low-fat milk
- 1 tablespoon sugar
- 1 pinch salt

Tools

- chef's knife
- cutting board
- grill
- tongs
- saucepan
- whisk

1 Slice the fruit into chunks for grilling.

2 To make each sauce, combine the ingredients in a saucepan. Bring to a simmer over medium heat. Reduce to low heat and whisk gently for 5 minutes. Store in separate thermoses to take to the stadium.

3 Heat the grill to 400ºF. Grill the fruit for about 3 minutes or until grill marks appear. Use tongs to remove safely.

4 Serve with ice cream and top with the sauce of your choice.

COACH'S TIP

Don't stop with sauces! Add sprinkles, cookie crumbles, or whipped cream to give the sundae your personal touch. Even better, top off your fruit sundae with more fruit—add a cherry!

CARAMEL BROWNIES

Hut! Hut! Hike … one of those brownies in my direction!

PREP TIME	15 MINUTES
COOK TIME	25 TO 30 MINUTES
SERVES	8 TO 10 PEOPLE

Tools

- measuring cups/ spoons
- mixing bowl
- scraper
- 8 x 8-inch baking dish
- saucepan
- whisk
- toothpick
- paring knife

Ingredients

- 1 cup flour
- 1 cup sugar
- ½ cup unsweetened cocoa powder
- 1 stick butter, melted
- 2 teaspoons vanilla extract
- 2 eggs
- ¼ cup water
- cooking spray
- 20 soft caramel candies, unwrapped
- ¼ cup sweetened condensed milk

1 Preheat oven to 350°F.

2 Combine the flour, sugar, cocoa powder, butter, vanilla extract, eggs, and water in a mixing bowl. Stir until most of the lumps of flour are dissolved.

CALL AN AUDIBLE

To add some crunch to your brownies, add ¼ cup chopped pecans after pouring the melted caramel in step 6. For an even sweeter result, add ½ cup chocolate chips or melted caramel on top of the brownies after step 8.

3 Spritz baking dish with cooking spray and pour three-fourths of the batter into the dish.

4 Place in the oven and bake for about 10 minutes.

5 Meanwhile, place the caramels and sweetened condensed milk in a saucepan and whisk slowly over low heat until the caramels melt.

6 Remove the baking dish from the oven and pour the melted caramels over the brownies.

7 Scrape the remaining brownie batter over the caramels and swirl the batter around using the scraper.

8 Return the baking dish to the oven for an additional 25 to 30 minutes or until a toothpick inserted into a brownie comes out clean.

9 Allow to cool for 30 minutes before cutting into squares.

STRAWBERRY SHORTCAKE ON A STICK

What do you get when you cross a classic dessert with a tailgating twist? A sweet shortcake on a stick!

PREP TIME	10 MINUTES
SERVES	8 PEOPLE

Tools

- cutting board
- paring knife
- chef's knife
- 8 8-inch wooden skewers

Ingredients

- 16-ounce container of strawberries
- 1 pound cake
- 1 7-ounce aerosol can whipped cream

CALL AN AUDIBLE

Mix up the flavor by subbing in different fruits. You can also use cookie cutters to create various shapes with the cake.

1 Cut off the top of each strawberry. Cut the strawberries into ½-inch thick rounds. If the strawberries are between ½ inch and 1 inch, just cut off the tops.

2 Cut the pound cake into four equal sections, lengthwise. Then cut each section into eight squares.

3 Thread one piece of cake onto a skewer, followed by a squirt of whipped cream, then a strawberry. Repeat one to three more times on each skewer. Serve immediately.

PUMPKIN MAPLE WHOOPIE PIES

Give your dessert a double-team of fall flavors! Both pumpkin and maple give these whoopie pies the perfect autumn taste.

PREP TIME	30 MINUTES
COOK TIME	15 MINUTES
MAKES	12 WHOOPIE PIES

Tools
- 2 baking sheets
- parchment paper
- 3 mixing bowls
- whisk
- large spoon
- spatula
- cooling rack
- electric hand mixer
- spoon

Ingredients

- 2 cups all-purpose flour
- 1 teaspoon baking powder
- 1 teaspoon baking soda
- 1 teaspoon ground cinnamon
- ½ teaspoon ground cloves
- ½ teaspoon kosher salt
- 1 stick butter, softened to room temperature
- 1 cup granulated sugar
- 2 large eggs
- 1 tablespoon vanilla extract
- 1 cup canned pumpkin, pureed

For the filling:

- 4 ounces cream cheese, softened to room temperature
- 3 tablespoons butter, softened to room temperature
- ½ teaspoon maple extract
- 2 tablespoons pure maple syrup
- 1 cup powdered sugar
- 1 0.68-ounce tube decorating gel

1 Preheat oven to 350ºF. Line baking sheets with parchment paper and set aside.

2 Combine the flour, baking powder, baking soda, cinnamon, cloves, and salt in a medium-sized mixing bowl. Set aside.

3 Beat the butter and sugar in a large mixing bowl with a whisk for 2 minutes. Add eggs, pumpkin, and vanilla. Beat until smooth.

4 Stir pumpkin mixture into the flour until it's mixed in thoroughly.

CALL AN AUDIBLE

If you don't like maple, you don't have to send this recipe to the locker room. Skip the extract and syrup and use 2 teaspoons of vanilla.

5 Using a large spoon, drop 24 scoops 1 inch apart on the baking sheets. Mold the scoops into ovals.

6 Bake for about 15 minutes.

7 Remove the baking sheets from the oven and allow to cool for 10 minutes. Then use a spatula to transfer the cookies to cooling racks.

8 Meanwhile, make the filling: Using a hand mixer, beat the cream cheese, butter, maple extract, and maple syrup on medium speed in a large mixing bowl until well combined.

9 Add a little powdered sugar at a time while mixing on low speed. After all the sugar is added, turn the mixer up to medium and mix until fluffy.

10 To assemble the whoopie pies, spread a heaping spoonful of filling on the flat side of one cookie. Top it off with another cookie, placing the flat side down. Use the gel to create laces on the top cookie. Repeat with the rest of the cookies.

11 Serve. Store leftovers in an airtight container in the refrigerator.

Whether it's a hot summer day or a cool fall evening, toast the big winners with these tempting tailgating thirst-quenchers.

POMEGRANATE LEMONADE

Tools
- measuring cup
- 2-quart pitcher
- spoon

Ingredients
- 1 quart prepared lemonade
- 1 cup pomegranate juice
- 3 cups seltzer water
- ice

Combine the lemonade, pomegranate juice, and seltzer in pitcher and stir gently. Serve over ice.

RASPBERRY-PINEAPPLE SPRITZER

Tools
- measuring cup
- blender
- 2-quart pitcher
- spoon

Ingredients
- 1 cup raspberries
- 1 quart pineapple juice
- 3 cups seltzer
- ice

Blend raspberries on high until pureed. Combine blended raspberries, pineapple juice, and seltzer in pitcher and stir gently. Serve over ice.

CRANBERRY-APPLE PUNCH

Tools
- measuring cup
- 2-quart pitcher
- spoon

Ingredients
- 3 cups apple cider
- 3 cups ginger ale
- 2 cups cranberry juice
- ice

Combine the apple cider, ginger ale, and cranberry juice in a pitcher and stir gently. Serve over ice.

CREAMY HOT CHOCOLATE

Tools
- 3-quart slow cooker
- measuring cups
- whisk
- ladle, for serving

Ingredients
- ½ cup unsweetened cocoa powder
- 1 14-ounce can sweetened condensed milk
- 8 cups milk
- 1 tablespoon vanilla
- 1 teaspoon cinnamon
- marshmallows or whipped cream, for topping

Combine first five ingredients in a slow cooker. Whisk until mostly dissolved. Cook on low for 3 hours. Serve hot with marshmallows or whipped cream.

GRILLED PIZZA

Put away your cell phone! You don't need to order out for pizza at your tailgating party. Prove that you're a cooking pro and create your own pizza combination with a hearty grilled taste.

PREP TIME	1 HOUR 30 MINUTES (1 HOUR INACTIVE)
COOK TIME	10 MINUTES
SERVES	6 PEOPLE

Tools

- measuring cups/ spoons
- 2 mixing bowls
- damp kitchen towel
- cutting board
- chef's knife
- grater
- rolling pin
- pizza stone
- grill
- pizza cutter

Ingredients

For the pizza dough:

- 1 teaspoon active dry yeast
- ½ teaspoon honey
- 1 pinch salt
- ¾ cup warm water
- 1½ cups all-purpose flour, plus extra for kneading
- 1 teaspoon olive oil

For the toppings:

- 1 teaspoon olive oil
- ½ cup pizza sauce
- 1½ cups mozzarella cheese
- 1 teaspoon dried basil
- your favorite toppings, such as pepperoni, cooked sausage, ham, mushrooms, onions, peppers, pineapple, or cheddar cheese

For the dough:

1 In a large mixing bowl, add the yeast, honey, salt, and water. Stir once thoroughly and allow to sit for about 10 minutes or until all of the ingredients have dissolved and bubbled.

2 Add flour to the bowl and use your hands to mix the ingredients well.

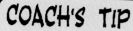

3 Sprinkle some flour on a clean surface and put the dough ball on it. Knead until the dough is soft and smooth, about 8 to 10 minutes. Add more flour to the surface if it starts to get too sticky.

4 Coat the inside of the second mixing bowl with the olive oil. Place the dough ball in the bowl and cover with a damp towel. Allow to rise for about an hour.

5 Meanwhile, get your toppings ready. Grate the cheese. Slice the meats and vegetables thinly so they cook quickly when the pizza is grilled. Set the toppings aside.

6 After the dough has finished rising, sprinkle flour on a flat surface. Place the dough in the flour. Give it a quick knead—just one or two times. Then put some flour on the rolling pin and roll the dough into the shape of the pizza stone. Coat the pizza stone with olive oil and place the dough on top of it.

7 Spoon the pizza sauce on the dough, using the back of the spoon to spread it to ½ inch from the edge.

8 Sprinkle about three-fourths of the cheese on top of the sauce. Place your toppings on the cheese. Be careful not to overload the pizza, or it may get soggy! Then add the rest of the cheese and the dried basil on top of the pizza.

CALL AN AUDIBLE

Go outside the playbook and make a white pizza! Instead of pizza sauce, drizzle ¼ cup olive oil and 1 teaspoon crushed garlic on the pizza dough before you pile on cheese and your favorite toppings.

9 Heat the grill to 450°F. Place the stone on the grill and close the lid. Grill for 8 to 10 minutes or until the crust is slightly browned and the cheese is bubbly.

10 Use the pizza cutter to slice into triangles and serve.

Besel, Jen. *Sweet Tooth! No-Bake Desserts to Make and Devour.* North Mankato, Minn.: Capstone Press, 2015.

Gold, Rozanne. *Eat Fresh Food: Awesome Recipes for Teen Chefs.* New York: Bloomsbury Children's Books, 2009.

Meachen Rau, Dana. *A Teen Guide to Fast, Delicious Dinners.* North Mankato, Minn.: Compass Point Books, 2011.

Pellman Good, Phyllis. *Fix-It and Forget-It Kids' Cookbook: 50 Favorite Recipes to Make in a Slow Cooker.* Intercourse, Pa.: Good Books, 2010.

INTERNET SITES

FactHound offers a safe, fun way to find Internet sites related to this book. All of the sites on FactHound have been researched by our staff.

Here's all you do:

Visit *www.facthound.com*

Type in this code: 9781491421376

About the Author

Katrina Jorgensen is a graduate of Le Cordon Bleu College of Culinary Arts. She enjoys creating new recipes and sharing them with friends and family. She lives in Rochester, Minnesota, with her husband, Tony, and dog, Max.